EMMANUEL JOSEPH

Balanced Believer, Merging Faith, Relationships, Career, and Entrepreneurship

Copyright © 2025 by Emmanuel Joseph

All rights reserved. No part of this publication may be reproduced, stored or transmitted in any form or by any means, electronic, mechanical, photocopying, recording, scanning, or otherwise without written permission from the publisher. It is illegal to copy this book, post it to a website, or distribute it by any other means without permission.

First edition

This book was professionally typeset on Reedsy.
Find out more at reedsy.com

Contents

1. Chapter 1 — 1
2. Chapter 1: The Foundation of Faith — 3
3. Chapter 2: Nurturing Relationships — 5
4. Chapter 3: Career with a Purpose — 7
5. Chapter 4: The Entrepreneurial Spirit — 9
6. Chapter 5: Integrating Faith and Career — 11
7. Chapter 6: Building Strong Family Bonds — 13
8. Chapter 7: Finding Harmony in Friendships — 15
9. Chapter 8: Balancing Work and Personal Life — 17
10. Chapter 9: Pursuing Personal Growth — 19
11. Chapter 10: Giving Back to the Community — 21
12. Chapter 11: Embracing Spiritual Practices — 23
13. Chapter 12: Living a Balanced Life — 25

Chapter 1

Introduction

In the hustle and bustle of modern life, balancing faith, relationships, career, and entrepreneurship can seem like a daunting task. Yet, it is a pursuit worth undertaking. The balanced believer understands that these aspects of life are not isolated but interconnected threads in the fabric of a fulfilling existence. This book explores the journey of integrating faith with every aspect of life, creating harmony and purpose.

Faith serves as the foundation, guiding believers through the complexities of relationships, career, and entrepreneurship. It instills a sense of purpose and resilience, helping individuals navigate challenges with grace and confidence. Relationships, whether familial, romantic, or platonic, provide emotional support and a sense of belonging, enriching the believer's life with love and connection.

A purposeful career is more than a means to an end; it's an expression of one's values and passions. The balanced believer seeks to create a positive impact through their work, fostering integrity and collaboration. Entrepreneurship offers a unique opportunity to innovate and contribute to the community, driven by a vision grounded in faith and ethical practices.

This book is a guide for those who aspire to live a balanced life, where faith, relationships, career, and entrepreneurship are harmoniously integrated. It provides practical insights and strategies to navigate the journey, offering inspiration and encouragement to embrace this holistic approach. By the end of this book, readers will be equipped with the tools to create a life that reflects their deepest values and aspirations—a life of balance and fulfillment.

2

Chapter 1: The Foundation of Faith

In the intricate tapestry of life, faith stands as the cornerstone upon which everything else is built. It's the spiritual compass guiding us through life's labyrinth. Faith isn't just a set of beliefs or rituals; it's an unwavering trust in the divine, a beacon of hope in the face of adversities. For a balanced believer, faith transcends the confines of religious practices, becoming a living, breathing force that shapes thoughts, actions, and decisions.

Faith influences every aspect of a believer's life. It instills a sense of purpose, helping individuals understand that they are part of a grander design. When challenges arise, faith provides the strength to persevere, knowing that every trial is a stepping stone to personal growth. It cultivates a sense of gratitude, prompting believers to appreciate the small miracles in their everyday lives. In essence, faith is the glue that holds together the diverse strands of existence.

Moreover, faith fosters a sense of community and belonging. Through shared beliefs and practices, individuals find solidarity with others, creating bonds that transcend social, economic, and cultural differences. These connections are crucial for emotional and psychological well-being, providing a support system in times of need. Faith communities often become a refuge, offering solace and encouragement in moments of doubt and despair.

Faith also plays a pivotal role in ethical decision-making. It serves as a moral compass, guiding believers to differentiate between right and wrong. This ethical framework becomes particularly crucial in today's fast-paced world, where moral dilemmas are commonplace. A balanced believer relies on their faith to make choices that align with their values, ensuring integrity and authenticity in all aspects of life.

Ultimately, the foundation of faith is about more than just personal belief; it's about living a life of purpose, gratitude, and integrity. It's about creating meaningful connections with others and contributing to the greater good. For the balanced believer, faith isn't a separate part of life—it's the very essence that permeates and enriches every experience.

3

Chapter 2: Nurturing Relationships

Relationships are the heartbeat of human existence, providing joy, support, and a sense of belonging. For the balanced believer, nurturing relationships is a priority, rooted in the understanding that love and compassion are central tenets of faith. Whether it's with family, friends, or a partner, these connections are vital for emotional and spiritual well-being.

In a family setting, relationships are built on mutual respect, trust, and open communication. Parents guide their children with love and wisdom, instilling values that will shape their future. Siblings support each other through life's ups and downs, creating a bond that withstands the test of time. For the balanced believer, family isn't just a biological construct; it's a sacred unit where love and faith are intertwined.

Friendships also play a significant role in a balanced life. True friends are those who stand by us, offering support, encouragement, and a listening ear. They celebrate our successes and help us navigate our failures. For the balanced believer, friendships are cherished gifts, nurtured with care and intention. These relationships are strengthened through shared experiences and common values, creating a deep sense of connection.

In romantic relationships, love is seen as a divine gift, a manifestation of the divine love that sustains all creation. Partners in a balanced relationship support each other's growth, both spiritually and personally. They communicate openly, resolve conflicts with grace, and strive to build a life that reflects their shared values. For the balanced believer, a romantic relationship isn't just about companionship; it's a partnership in which both individuals grow together in faith and love.

However, nurturing relationships isn't without its challenges. Misunderstandings, conflicts, and differences in opinion are inevitable. The balanced believer approaches these challenges with patience, empathy, and a willingness to understand the other person's perspective. They prioritize forgiveness and reconciliation, recognizing that these are essential for maintaining healthy relationships.

Ultimately, nurturing relationships requires effort, commitment, and a genuine desire to connect with others on a deeper level. For the balanced believer, these relationships are a reflection of their faith and love for the divine. They understand that by loving and caring for others, they are fulfilling a fundamental aspect of their faith and enriching their own lives in the process.

4

Chapter 3: Career with a Purpose

In the pursuit of a fulfilling life, a career holds a significant place. For the balanced believer, a career isn't just a means to earn a living; it's an avenue to live out one's faith and make a positive impact on the world. It's about finding a vocation that aligns with one's values and passions, and that contributes to the greater good.

A career with a purpose starts with self-awareness. The balanced believer takes time to understand their strengths, interests, and values. They seek a career that allows them to utilize their talents in a meaningful way. This self-awareness ensures that their work is not just a job but a calling that brings fulfillment and joy.

Integrity is a cornerstone of a purposeful career. The balanced believer conducts themselves with honesty and fairness, even when faced with ethical dilemmas. They understand that their actions reflect their faith, and they strive to make decisions that align with their values. This integrity builds trust and respect among colleagues and clients, creating a positive work environment.

Collaboration and teamwork are also vital aspects of a career with a purpose. The balanced believer recognizes that they are part of a larger community, and they value the contributions of others. They work collaboratively, fostering a spirit of cooperation and mutual respect. This collaborative approach enhances productivity and creates a supportive work culture.

Moreover, the balanced believer seeks opportunities to give back through their career. Whether it's mentoring younger colleagues, volunteering for community projects, or advocating for social justice, they use their skills and resources to make a positive impact. They understand that their career is a platform to serve others and to contribute to the greater good.

In essence, a career with a purpose is about more than just professional success; it's about making a meaningful contribution to the world. For the balanced believer, their career is an expression of their faith and values. They strive to create a legacy that reflects their commitment to integrity, collaboration, and service.

5

Chapter 4: The Entrepreneurial Spirit

Entrepreneurship is a path that offers immense potential for personal and professional growth. For the balanced believer, it's an opportunity to create something meaningful, to innovate, and to make a positive impact. The entrepreneurial journey is guided by faith, resilience, and a commitment to ethical practices.

The entrepreneurial spirit begins with a vision. The balanced believer has a clear sense of purpose and a desire to solve problems or meet needs in the community. This vision is grounded in their values and driven by a passion for making a difference. It's a vision that inspires and motivates them to take bold steps and to overcome challenges.

Resilience is a crucial trait for entrepreneurs. The journey is often fraught with uncertainties, setbacks, and failures. The balanced believer draws strength from their faith, knowing that each setback is an opportunity for growth. They persevere with determination and optimism, confident that their efforts will bear fruit in due time.

Ethical practices are non-negotiable for the balanced entrepreneur. They conduct their business with honesty, fairness, and transparency. They treat employees, customers, and partners with respect and integrity. These ethical practices build trust and loyalty, creating a strong foundation for long-term success.

Innovation is at the heart of entrepreneurship. The balanced believer embraces creativity and is open to new ideas and approaches. They seek innovative solutions to address challenges and to create value. This innovative mindset enables them to stay ahead of the curve and to adapt to changing market dynamics.

Ultimately, the entrepreneurial journey is about more than just financial success; it's about creating a positive impact and leaving a lasting legacy. For the balanced believer, entrepreneurship is a way to live out their faith and values. They understand that their business can be a force for good, contributing to the well-being of the community and the world at large.

6

Chapter 5: Integrating Faith and Career

For the balanced believer, faith isn't confined to personal life; it extends to the professional realm as well. Integrating faith and career means bringing one's values and beliefs into the workplace and using them to guide decisions and actions. It's about creating harmony between one's spiritual and professional life.

One of the key aspects of integrating faith and career is authenticity. The balanced believer is true to their values, regardless of the circumstances. They don't compartmentalize their faith; instead, they allow it to permeate every aspect of their work. This authenticity creates a sense of integrity and trustworthiness that is essential for professional success.

Ethical decision-making is another crucial aspect. The balanced believer uses their faith as a moral compass, guiding them to make choices that align with their values. They prioritize honesty, fairness, and compassion in their interactions with colleagues, clients, and stakeholders. This ethical approach fosters a positive work environment and builds strong relationships.

Work-life balance is also essential for integrating faith and career. The balanced believer understands the importance of rest, reflection, and spiritual nourishment. They prioritize self-care and set boundaries to ensure that their professional responsibilities don't overshadow their personal and spiritual life. This balance enhances overall well-being and productivity.

Moreover, the balanced believer seeks to make a positive impact through their work. They use their skills and resources to contribute to the greater good, whether through community service, philanthropy, or social entrepreneurship. They understand that their career is a platform to live out their faith and to make a difference in the world.

In essence, integrating faith and career is about creating harmony and alignment between one's spiritual and professional life. For the balanced believer, it's a way to live authentically and to use their work as a means to serve others and to fulfill their divine purpose.

7

Chapter 6: Building Strong Family Bonds

Family is the bedrock of a balanced believer's life. Strong family bonds provide emotional support, a sense of belonging, and a foundation of love and faith. Building and maintaining these bonds requires intentionality, effort, and a commitment to nurturing relationships.

Communication is the cornerstone of strong family bonds. Open, honest, and respectful communication fosters understanding and trust. Family members should feel comfortable expressing their thoughts, feelings, and concerns without fear of judgment. The balanced believer prioritizes regular, meaningful conversations that strengthen connections and resolve conflicts.

Quality time is also essential for building strong family bonds. In today's fast-paced world, it's easy to become disconnected. The balanced believer makes a conscious effort to spend quality time with family members, whether it's through shared activities, meals, or simply being present. These moments create lasting memories and deepen emotional connections.

Support and encouragement are vital components of a strong family. Family members should be each other's biggest cheerleaders, offering support in times of need and celebrating successes together. The balanced believer creates a nurturing environment where each family member feels valued and appreciated.

Faith plays a significant role in building strong family bonds. Shared spiritual practices, such as prayer, worship, and religious traditions, create a sense of unity and purpose. For the balanced believer, faith is a source of strength and guidance, helping the family navigate challenges and grow together in love and spirituality.

Conflict resolution is another important aspect of building strong family bonds. Disagreements and misunderstandings are inevitable, but they should be addressed with patience, empathy, and a willingness to find common ground. The balanced believer prioritizes forgiveness and reconciliation, understanding that these are essential for maintaining healthy and harmonious relationships.

In essence, building strong family bonds requires effort, commitment, and a genuine desire to connect with and support each other. For the balanced believer, family is a reflection of their faith and love, and they strive to create a loving, supportive, and spiritually enriched family environment.

8

Chapter 7: Finding Harmony in Friendships

Friendships are an integral part of a balanced believer's life. They provide companionship, support, and opportunities for personal growth. Finding harmony in friendships involves nurturing these relationships with care, respect, and a commitment to shared values.

Trust and loyalty are the foundation of lasting friendships. Friends should be able to rely on each other, knowing that they have each other's best interests at heart. The balanced believer cultivates trust by being honest, dependable, and supportive. Loyalty ensures that friendships endure through both good times and bad.

Mutual respect is essential for harmonious friendships. Friends should appreciate each other's differences and celebrate their unique qualities. The balanced believer values diversity and approaches friendships with an open mind and heart. They understand that true friendship is built on mutual respect and acceptance.

Quality time is crucial for maintaining strong friendships. The balanced believer makes an effort to spend time with friends, engaging in activities that bring joy and create shared experiences. Whether it's a casual coffee chat, a weekend getaway, or a shared hobby, these moments strengthen the bond between friends.

Effective communication is key to harmonious friendships. Friends should feel comfortable expressing their thoughts, feelings, and concerns. The balanced believer prioritizes open and honest communication, addressing misunderstandings and conflicts with empathy and understanding. This approach fosters deeper connections and ensures that friendships remain strong and healthy.

Support and encouragement are vital components of true friendship. Friends should be each other's sources of motivation and inspiration. The balanced believer offers a listening ear, a shoulder to lean on, and words of encouragement. They celebrate their friends' successes and provide support during challenging times, creating a sense of camaraderie and mutual growth.

In essence, finding harmony in friendships requires effort, commitment, and a genuine desire to connect with and support each other. For the balanced believer, friendships are a reflection of their faith and values, and they strive to create meaningful, supportive, and enriching friendships that stand the test of time.

9

Chapter 8: Balancing Work and Personal Life

Finding a balance between work and personal life is a common challenge in today's fast-paced world. For the balanced believer, achieving this balance is essential for overall well-being and fulfillment. It involves setting boundaries, prioritizing self-care, and creating harmony between professional responsibilities and personal pursuits.

Setting boundaries is a crucial step in balancing work and personal life. The balanced believer understands the importance of defining clear limits between work and personal time. They establish boundaries to ensure that work doesn't encroach on personal life and vice versa. This approach helps create a healthy work-life balance and prevents burnout.

Time management is another essential aspect of balancing work and personal life. The balanced believer prioritizes tasks, sets realistic goals, and manages their time effectively. They allocate dedicated time for work, family, friends, and self-care, ensuring that each aspect of life receives the attention it deserves.

Self-care is vital for maintaining balance. The balanced believer recognizes the importance of taking care of their physical, mental, and emotional well-being. They prioritize activities that promote relaxation, rejuvenation, and overall health. This may include exercise, meditation, hobbies, or simply spending time in nature. Self-care enhances overall well-being and productivity.

Flexibility is also key to achieving balance. The balanced believer understands that life is unpredictable, and flexibility is essential for navigating changing circumstances. They adapt to new situations with grace and resilience, finding creative solutions to maintain balance. This flexibility allows them to thrive in both their professional and personal life.

Moreover, the balanced believer seeks to integrate their faith into their daily routine. They find moments for reflection, prayer, and spiritual nourishment, even amidst a busy schedule. This integration of faith provides a sense of grounding and purpose, helping them maintain balance and harmony in their life.

In essence, balancing work and personal life requires intentionality, effort, and a commitment to self-care and well-being. For the balanced believer, this balance is essential for living a fulfilling and meaningful life. They strive to create harmony between their professional responsibilities and personal pursuits, ensuring that each aspect of life is enriched and nurtured.

10

Chapter 9: Pursuing Personal Growth

Personal growth is a lifelong journey for the balanced believer. It involves continuous learning, self-improvement, and a commitment to becoming the best version of oneself. Pursuing personal growth requires intentionality, reflection, and a willingness to embrace change and challenges.

Self-awareness is the foundation of personal growth. The balanced believer takes time to understand their strengths, weaknesses, and areas for improvement. They engage in self-reflection and seek feedback from others to gain insight into their behavior and mindset. This self-awareness allows them to make informed decisions and take deliberate steps toward personal growth.

Continuous learning is essential for personal growth. The balanced believer values education and seeks opportunities to expand their knowledge and skills. They engage in activities that stimulate their mind, such as reading, attending workshops, or pursuing new hobbies. This commitment to learning keeps them intellectually engaged and opens doors to new possibilities.

Embracing change is a crucial aspect of personal growth. The balanced believer understands that growth often involves stepping out of their comfort zone and embracing new experiences. They approach change with an open mind and a positive attitude, seeing it as an opportunity for growth and transformation. This mindset allows them to navigate challenges and uncertainties with resilience and grace.

Setting goals is also important for personal growth. The balanced believer sets realistic and meaningful goals that align with their values and aspirations. They create a roadmap for achieving these goals and take consistent action toward them. This goal-setting process provides a sense of direction and motivation, helping them stay focused on their growth journey.

Moreover, the balanced believer prioritizes self-care and well-being. They understand that personal growth is not just about achieving external success but also about nurturing their inner self. They engage in activities that promote mental, emotional, and spiritual well-being, such as meditation, journaling, or spending time in nature. This holistic approach enhances their overall growth and fulfillment.

In essence, pursuing personal growth is about continuous learning, embracing change, and nurturing one's well-being. For the balanced believer, personal growth is a lifelong journey that enriches their life and allows them to become the best version of themselves. They strive to create a fulfilling and meaningful life through intentional growth and self-improvement.

11

Chapter 10: Giving Back to the Community

Giving back to the community is a fundamental aspect of the balanced believer's life. It involves using one's skills, resources, and time to make a positive impact on others. For the balanced believer, giving back is an expression of their faith and values, and it enhances their sense of purpose and fulfillment.

Volunteering is one way to give back to the community. The balanced believer seeks opportunities to serve others, whether it's through local organizations, charities, or community projects. They dedicate their time and effort to causes that align with their values and passions. Volunteering not only benefits the community but also provides a sense of fulfillment and connection.

Philanthropy is another important aspect of giving back. The balanced believer uses their financial resources to support causes that make a difference. Whether it's donating to a charity, funding a scholarship, or supporting a community project, their contributions create a positive impact. Philanthropy allows them to use their resources for the greater good and to create a lasting legacy.

Mentorship is also a valuable way to give back. The balanced believer shares their knowledge, experience, and guidance with others, helping them navigate their own journey. They offer support and encouragement, helping others achieve their goals and reach their potential. Mentorship creates a ripple effect, as those who receive support are often inspired to give back in turn.

Advocacy is another powerful way to contribute to the community. The balanced believer advocates for social justice, equality, and positive change. They use their voice to raise awareness about important issues and to promote solutions that benefit the community. Advocacy allows them to make a difference and to create a more just and compassionate world.

Ultimately, giving back to the community is about using one's skills, resources, and time to make a positive impact and creating a lasting legacy. For the balanced believer, giving back is a reflection of their faith and values, and it enriches their own life as well.

12

Chapter 11: Embracing Spiritual Practices

Spiritual practices are essential for nurturing faith and maintaining a balanced life. For the balanced believer, these practices provide moments of reflection, connection, and spiritual nourishment. Embracing spiritual practices involves integrating them into daily life and creating a routine that supports spiritual growth.

Prayer is a fundamental spiritual practice for the balanced believer. It provides a way to communicate with the divine, seeking guidance, strength, and comfort. Regular prayer fosters a sense of connection and trust in the divine, helping the believer navigate life's challenges with faith and resilience. Whether it's through structured prayers or spontaneous conversations with the divine, prayer is a source of spiritual nourishment.

Meditation is another valuable spiritual practice. It offers a way to quiet the mind, reflect, and connect with the inner self. The balanced believer embraces meditation as a means to cultivate mindfulness, clarity, and inner peace. Regular meditation practice enhances mental and emotional well-being, providing a sense of grounding and balance.

Reading and studying sacred texts is also an important spiritual practice. For the balanced believer, these texts provide wisdom, inspiration, and guidance. Regular study of sacred texts deepens understanding of faith and fosters spiritual growth. It offers insights into ethical and moral principles, helping the believer make decisions that align with their values.

Community worship is another valuable aspect of spiritual practice. The balanced believer participates in communal worship, whether it's through religious services, prayer groups, or faith-based gatherings. These communal experiences create a sense of unity and support, fostering connections with others who share similar beliefs and values.

Moreover, the balanced believer embraces acts of service as a spiritual practice. Serving others is a way to live out faith and to contribute to the greater good. Whether it's through volunteering, philanthropy, or simple acts of kindness, service enriches the spiritual life and creates a positive impact on the community.

In essence, embracing spiritual practices is about integrating them into daily life and creating a routine that supports spiritual growth. For the balanced believer, these practices provide moments of reflection, connection, and nourishment, helping them maintain a balanced and fulfilling life.

13

Chapter 12: Living a Balanced Life

Living a balanced life is the ultimate goal for the balanced believer. It involves integrating faith, relationships, career, and entrepreneurship in a way that creates harmony and fulfillment. It requires intentionality, effort, and a commitment to living authentically and purposefully.

Self-awareness is the foundation of a balanced life. The balanced believer takes time to understand their values, strengths, and areas for improvement. They engage in self-reflection and seek feedback to gain insight into their behavior and mindset. This self-awareness allows them to make informed decisions and take deliberate steps toward a balanced life.

Setting priorities is essential for achieving balance. The balanced believer understands the importance of defining clear priorities and allocating time and resources accordingly. They create a roadmap for achieving their goals and maintaining harmony between different aspects of life. This approach helps create a sense of direction and focus.

Flexibility is also key to living a balanced life. The balanced believer understands that life is unpredictable, and flexibility is essential for navigating changing circumstances. They adapt to new situations with grace and resilience, finding creative solutions to maintain balance. This flexibility allows them to thrive in both their personal and professional life.

Self-care is vital for maintaining balance. The balanced believer prioritizes activities that promote physical, mental, and emotional well-being. They engage in practices such as exercise, meditation, hobbies, or spending time in nature. Self-care enhances overall well-being and productivity, ensuring that they have the energy and resilience to meet life's demands.

Ultimately, living a balanced life is about creating harmony and alignment between different aspects of life. For the balanced believer, it's a way to live authentically and purposefully, using their faith, relationships, career, and entrepreneurship to create a fulfilling and meaningful life. They strive to maintain balance through intentionality, effort, and a commitment to living in accordance with their values.

Book Description:

In a world that often pulls us in many directions, maintaining a balance between faith, relationships, career, and entrepreneurship can be challenging. **"Balanced Believer: Merging Faith, Relationships, Career, and Entrepreneurship"** offers a comprehensive guide for those seeking harmony in their lives.

This book delves into the essence of what it means to be a balanced believer. It explores the foundation of faith, the importance of nurturing relationships, the pursuit of a purposeful career, and the spirit of entrepreneurship. Each chapter provides practical insights, actionable strategies, and inspirational stories to help readers integrate these aspects of life seamlessly.

Through thoughtful reflections and real-life examples, the book illustrates how faith can be a guiding force in all endeavors, how strong relationships can provide unwavering support, how a career can be an expression of one's values, and how entrepreneurship can be a pathway to positive impact.

"Balanced Believer" is not just a guide but a companion on the journey to living a fulfilling and meaningful life. It empowers readers to embrace their faith, foster meaningful connections, pursue their passions, and create a legacy that reflects their deepest values. Whether you're just starting out or seeking to realign your life, this book provides the wisdom and encouragement needed to navigate the complexities of modern life with grace and purpose.

www.ingramcontent.com/pod-product-compliance
Lightning Source LLC
Chambersburg PA
CBHW072023290426
44109CB00018B/2327